YOUR LIFE
OF PERSONAL
POWER

YOUR LIFE
OF PERSONAL
POWER

20 LESSONS
TO EMPOWER YOU

ANNA M. WILLIAMS
Modern Mystic

London

Your Life of Personal Power: 20 Lessons to Empower You

The information given in this book should not be treated as a substitute for professional medical advice. Always consult a medical practitioner.

Although the author and publisher have made every effort to ensure that the information in this book was correct at press time, the author and publisher do not assume and hereby disclaim any liability to any party for any loss, damage, or disruption caused by errors or omissions, whether such errors or omissions result from negligence, accident, or any other cause.

The book information is catalogued as follows;
Author Name(s): Anna M. Williams
Title: Your Life of Personal Power: 20 Lessons to Empower You

Description; First Edition

1st Edition, 2021

Book Design by Leah Kent

ISBN 978-1-914447-02-0 (paperback)
ISBN 978-1-914447-03-7 (ebook)

Published by That Guy's House
www.ThatGuysHouse.com

First I would like to dedicate this book to all my children and grandchildren. Be you even when others don't agree, including me!

Next to all my readers: be you, be true to yourself and be authentic in all that you do.

CONTENTS

Introduction

Over the last six years, I have noticed a vast amount of people I work with do not pursue their passion or true desires in life. I cannot tell you how many times I have heard an individual say they aren't able to do something because they are too old, not talented enough, not smart enough, or they worry about what others will think.

I went back to school at the age of 44 years old. There were many people in my classes that were older than the typical college student. Even when my middle daughter went to college, she said she was surprised at how many of her classmates were older than her. She mentioned that she expected more people her age. I personally believe that you are never too old to learn something new – even if it is nothing more than for your entertainment or because you thirst for knowledge.

After a little while, I really started to notice that the people I work with and even family and friends do not pursue their dreams at all, or they keep their ambitions and aspirations a secret to only a few people they can trust without fear of being criticized or made fun of.

This book is for those who often feel restricted or unable to do the things they truly desire because of the circumstances and restrictions of our modern-day society and/or their culture. It is for those who have been told that they are not able or worthy enough to do or be who they really desire or aspire to be or do. My hope is this book will help others to recognize not only their own ambitions, desires and dreams but also to achieve them. They have the personal power to change their lives and to accomplish the things they truly want in life, rather than to allow their life to be dictated by others.

Assisting others to realize that they are capable and actually have their own personal power has also helped me to realize where I, too, have been holding back in many areas of my life. My hope in writing this book is that I am able to reach a larger group of individuals who are able to recognize that they are more than capable of going after and achieving both their dreams and desires to a more fulfilling life.

I have lived and fought to take back my own personal power to do and accomplish the things that really matter to me. Not only for myself but to also be living proof that other people do not get to dictate your life and how you live it.

I want my readers to know they, too, can accomplish and live their lives on their own terms. I want them to feel empowered to make their own decisions regardless of how or what others may think. There is power in creating your own path, being who you are, and being different.

So, yes, I am who I am. I am different. If you do not agree with who I am, I bless you with lots of love and light and wish you well on your journey in life. If you like what you see or are curious, then take my hand, and we will see where all of this takes us.

Much love always,
Modern Mystic

What is Personal Power?

As babies, we are all born with our own personal power. All of it without limitations. However, usually starting in early childhood, we are taught there are things that we are not able to do or should not do because of who we are or who others think we should be.

As young children, many of us were told our dreams were not possible because of our gender, social status, or even because of a disability. There are many people that have achieved their dreams despite what they have been told. Some of those who have succeeded have turned around and assisted others in reaching for their dreams as well.

We knew nothing of gender roles, cultural restrictions or limitations and how western society places those on us as we grow. Most people are unaware growing up that they even have personal power, and they are able or have a choice to do the things they desire.

I started to think I had no personal power when I was about nine years old, when my older brothers would not let me play football or other "boys only" things that they did. As I got older, it continued with school, where the girls were encouraged to learn to cook and sew, because that was what girls were supposed to do. Girls were not encouraged to take shop class, for example, because it was a "boy's class."

Even when I joined the military, there were many who did not understand why a girl would want to join the military service, because that is what boys do. They essentially were saying the military was not for women, and only men should serve our country.

Throughout this book, I will give many more examples of how our society has made us believe that we as individuals do not have any personal power, and we should follow and do only what is acceptable.

I will also provide some questions for reflection at the end of each chapter. I encourage you to write the answers in your journal, as this will help you to look deep within yourself to find and recognize the answers that are true for you. You can also look back on your answers later on and see just how far you've come!

My hope is that you take this book and use the lessons in it to help you not only recognize where you have been told you do not have personal power but to also show you that you can reclaim your personal power, like I did myself. So many in the world are tired of being told we are not good enough or strong enough or that our desires are not valid. It's time to make a change and take back our personal power.

1

Made to Feel Unworthy

We are taught at a young age how society determines what social class you are in and what is expected of you because of where they have placed each of us. Family and friends also try to tell us our worth in many different ways. Gender roles are another way society and families create feelings of unworthiness in others.

Society has become a hierarchy that people have let determine who they are and what they are able to archive. I will cover this more in a later chapter on success.

Family – this might be a touchy subject for many, and for others, it may be an eye-opener. In some cultures, people are taught to honor their family or traditions and deny who they are or what they want in life. Many cultures bind people to others by promising to do or not to do something. An example of this would be if a parent who is very ill and is not expected to live asked a child to honor them by taking care of other family members, instead of living the life the child truly desire. To not keep the promise would be to dishonor oneself, which is meant to make the child feel unworthy if they do not honor their parents' wishes.

I have witnessed this many times in movies and in real life. In some movies, it is depicted that if someone dishonors their family, it brings shame among the family as a whole. It is often used as a control tactic. In real life, it is often the oldest or youngest who is made to believe they are responsible for other family members and are often criticized for wanting more or something different.

I have also observed family members degrade others in the family for something as simple as arriving at a family reunion with new shoes by saying, "Who do you think you are showing up here with those new, bright white shoes?" Really?! What does having new shoes have to do with enjoying the time spent with other family members who you have not seen in a while? Does it really matter that I have new shoes? And how does a new pair of shoes make me better than you? I have come to realize that this person was trying to undermine my worthiness by trying to make me feel bad for having something new because they felt they could not afford to purchase some-thing as basic as new shoes. The odd part was the shoes I had bought cost only about $5. It was not like I was wearing an expense pair of shoes that had cost me hundreds of dollars. I have witnessed many people demean others as a way to pick away at their self-confidence and to make them feel unworthy, essentially saying, "How dare you be more success-ful or have more than me?"

Worthiness is defined by a person's perception and what we are taught while growing up. We are often taught that whether or not we are worthy of love, success, happiness, jobs, homes, vehicles and health depends how good of a person we are. We are considered good if we follow all the rules and do everything that we are told. If we deviate from those rules, we are often considered unworthy of things.

"Gaslighting" is another way another someone may try to make you doubt yourself, which eats away at your confidence. Gaslighting is typically done by someone telling you something and then later saying they did not say it. It can make you feel like you are crazy and really can make you question your-self. I had an ex-husband who would do this to me. He would tell me little things and then later say he never said it. I would get really pissed off because I knew he had said it. After a little while, I would notice that he would get a smirk on his face when I would get upset. After a while, I stopped confronting him because I realized that is what he wanted. He wanted me to question what I was being told so it would throw me off balance to what I knew to be true. By keeping me off balance, he was trying to gain control over my confidence and make me feel unworthy by way of second-guessing my thinking.

If you pay attention, you notice the beauty industry shows men and women who are young, very attractive, and skinny to tell you that you need this or that product to be desirable to the opposite sex or to be successful in any area of your life. If you look around you, you can see how those around you will constantly change their appearance based on what actors or the beauty industry is telling them they should do. This really struck me one day when I was working with a woman who mentioned "the people in Hollywood" were not tanning anymore, and that she was upset because she had started tanning. It confounded me for a little bit way it would matter what the people in Hollywood were doing until I realized she was trying to appear successful or worthy by doing the things that she considered to be successful by others. She was letting others determine how and what she needed to do to be worthy of success.

Women are expected to be tall, slim and beautiful before they are considered desirable or attractive to men. Again.... Really?! Beauty comes in all shapes and sizes. Some men like women that are a little "thick" in the thighs. Men are measured on how "ripped" they are. They have to have a six-pack on their stomachs to be thought of as "hot." Again, the general public is measuring a person's worthiness by the way they physically look.

Gender roles are another way society has pro-grammed the populace with what is acceptable and what is not. Men are not supposed to play with dolls. How are men supposed to learn to take care of a child if he is now allowed to play and learn? Same for women, how are women supposed to learn if they are not allowed to get dirty playing outside or to help in the garage with changing the engine oil of a car/truck? Men are not seen as "manly" if they like to do things that are considered "women's work." Women are not looked at as "feminine" if they are doing something that is looked at as a "man's job." Society has taught us that men are not worthy of being called a man if he stays home and takes care of the children just as much as women are looked down upon if they do not want children.

Redefine for yourself what you are worthy of, who you are and what you consider to be an achievement.

If all you ever wanted when you grew up was to be a CEO of a large corporation and you obtain it, then, of course, you would consider yourself successful. Yet if all you ever wanted to be since you were little was to be a parent and you have a family now, then, YES, you are also successful, and you have accomplished that which you most desired in life. You get to determine for yourself what is considered to be successful or an achievement, not somebody else.

Those who feel like they do not have enough of something will oftentimes try to make you feel unworthy, so you do not turn out to be or have more than they do. They need you to feel small, so they will feel powerful and feel better about themselves. Many have feelings of not being worthy enough because others have possessions they desperately want but do not have or are unable to acquire.

Worthiness comes from inside. Ensure the things you desire are things that you truly want and are not based on society's definition of success. You can define your worth, or you can believe what someone else to define your worth.

Journal Questions

- Try journaling about the various ways that you have been told or made to feel like you do not deserve even the smallest of things in your life.

- Have you ever felt or told that you were asking for too much? Or that you do not deserve that which you truly desire?

- Have you ever been told or made to feel like you should not want something because others will have less than you? Are you really asking for too much, so others do not think you have more than them?

- Has anyone criticized you for having something only because they do not have or are unable to afford things, even little things that you may possess?

2

Be Different

We all want to feel we belong in the world. We want to be accepted and liked as well as appreciated for who we are. Yet we are all so very different in many different ways.

We may come from a large family or a very small community. It really does not matter where we come from, but we long to know that we are accepted or loved.

We play games with other children. We study the homework the teacher gives us in hopes that we get good grades to make our parents happy and hope they are proud of us.

Following the rules may work for many different things, yet sometimes those same things we know are not what we truly know or what makes us happy.

In adolescence, we often will do what everyone else is doing to help us fit in. Most are afraid to be different because they want to have friends and to be liked by their peers. I understand this all too well. I can remember growing up that those kids (me included) who did not have the most stylish clothes were often looked down on. Even in high school, when I would wear something that was slightly different from what others were wearing, I would get funny looks or made fun of. For many years, I let others dictate what type of clothes I should wear. What made it even worse was I would oftentimes feel uncomfortable when I would wear something that I did like that was stylish because I was treated like I was not "wealthy enough."

I was taught that in school that I was part of a certain class of society, and if I were to try to be other than who others thought I should be, I was looked down upon. Again, I was letting others decide who I should be. In reality, I have come to realize that just because I am different does not make me less of a person or less worthy of all there is in this life. I wear clothes that make me feel comfortable and stylish no matter what others think, including items that others would not consider normal. I like to oftentimes just throw on something fun and maybe a little funky just to be different and to show others that they, too, can have fun and be different.

This same concept can be applied to many different areas of your life. For example, I have applied the same thing to my hair. I have only a few occasions highlighted my hair. I am not one to constantly color my hair to look younger or more stylish. I prefer to celebrate my age by letting my hair be natural and letting it go grey without an apology. Yes, I am getting older, but you know what? I don't care!

I love getting older because I know all too well that there are many people who have not made it to my age. Too many others have died way too young. So yes, I prefer to celebrate getting older because I get to spend each and every day with those that I love and doing what I love.

I challenge you: Dare to be Different, even if it is in a small way. Be weird so others will feel empowered to also be weird. Even it is just a little. Adding or doing little things that say, "Yes I am different, I'm doing what I want, and so can you," such as a funky pair of shoes, a streak of color in your hair or even a fun handbag, can really make you feel alive. Guys, you can do things to be different too. Maybe there is a special type of hat that you like. I knew one fellow that liked to wear some fun or funky socks. Shoes? Belts? Sunglasses? Hawaiian shirts?! How about taking an art class or even an acting class? Do you like to write? Have you always wanted to learn how to play an instrument? Oh! How about taking dance classes?

Remember, others that make fun or criticize often lack the courage to be different. That is their issue, not yours.

Journal Questions

- Journal times in your life where you were either made fun of, or someone may have criticized for you being different.

- Do you like clothes that are not considered 'normal'? Does it really matter what you wear as an individual to show your own style? Is it because is it either more expensive or because it was purchased as a second-hand store?

- Do social classes in society determine or define who you need to be? Just because someone has things that are more expensive does not mean they are better than those who chose to purchase more affordable items.

3

Give Until it Hurts … Not!

While at work one day, one of my co-workers was telling me about a pastor that visited their church last Sunday and talked about tithing and giving until it hurts. Supposedly it's not about the money, yet the pastor kept referring to giving more money to the church…What?!

Here in the United States, many of the churches tell their congregation that they are not Christian or of service to God unless they give (money) until it hurts. Why would God want you to suffer by giving the church money until it hurts? The Bible talks about tithing and giving back to those less fortunate. For me, giving should be joyful and from the heart. Giving from pain is not joyful and feels more like obligation (giving away something you do not want to give).

My coworker went on to say how the pastor told stories of giving less to those we love but being more generous to ourselves or strangers. She stated how the pastor used an example of a man telling his people to give him money so he could buy a new suit because he was going on a business trip and how he would buy the most expensive food at a restaurant because "he does not get to eat like this every day." All the stories she repeated were about giving money… until it hurts. Again, the pastor stated it was not about the money but about being of service.

Why would I give from a place of hurt? Giving until it hurts is giving your power away. It is doing something that is painful. Giving when it hurts does not make you feel powerful. Why give until it hurts if it is only because someone else says it is the only way to be Christ-like (or a good person, Godly, etc.)?

Now I understand the Bible teaches us to be of service to others and tithe, but tithing can be many things, not just money. Merriam-Webster defines "tithe" as "a tenth part of something paid as a voluntary contribution or as a tax, especially for the support for a religious establishment." While churches need money to pay for the building and expenses of maintaining the utilities, I find it frustrating the religious leaders take advantage of their people by convincing them the only way to be of service is to give money (especially if they say give till it hurts).

It's frustrating to watch people like my coworker who says she does not have much money to give and is made to feel guilty or that they are not being of service to God if they are not giving more money than they can really afford.

The Bible says we are born to live an abundant life. Abundance can be in many forms, not just an abundance of money. There are many who have an abundance of time and skills as we all have talents and gifts that can be used to help others without causing pain and hurt to ourselves.

Being made to feel obligated or guilty is giving away your power to another. Kindness, generosity, joy and love starts with yourself. Tithing (giving) to others should come from your abundance. While sometimes you may have more money than you do have time, true power comes from giving only when your cup is overflowing, not from when it is almost empty. Giving should be joyful, not only for others who are receiving the giving but also joyful for you, and it should truly come from the heart with love and compassion, not from pain and discomfort or guilt.

I have learnt over the years that when you give from the heart with love (not hurt), whatever it is you are giving is more meaningful for both you and the person you are giving to. True tithing includes much more than money, time or talent … it is an abundance that is given with love.

Journal Questions

- Why are we made to feel like giving has to hurt?

- Does being generous have to be painful? Why or why not?

- What other ways can you find to give that do not include money? Time? Service to others? What items do you have that you no longer need that someone else could use?

4

Sexuality

Oh no! She did not go there? LOL. Yes, I am going there. Sex and sexuality in most societies are considered "no-no subjects" or taboo. I think the biggest reason most people are uncomfortable talking about sex and sexuality is that we have been given information that is based in fear and/or ego. Men and women are given different standards. Shame and guilt are placed on children and teenagers. Homosexuality is not accepted in most cultures and religions. It is no wonder there are so many people who are sexually dysfunctional and lash out because they do not know how to express their sensuality and sexuality.

Men and women are held to different standards when it comes to having sex. We live in a male-dominated world. Men are taught that they are not real men unless they have "sown their oats" with many women. Men feel their masculinity is based on how many women they've had sex with or how often they have sex. Women have been taught they should be ashamed of their bodies because their bodies give men "sinful" thoughts. Girls are told if they have sex with many different partners, then they are considered "whores" or called "sluts." So, it is said that men can have lots of sexual partners, but women cannot. Really? Why not?

We are made from sex. Having sex is a natural part of who we are. All animals in nature have sex. Without sex, every species alive would not survive. Sex is a part of life. If we look at it as a natural part of who we are, I think we would all be more comfortable and confident in ourselves. Having a healthy sexuality is a vital part of who we are as people.

Many religions teach us that we are to save ourselves for the one and only person we are to marry. Umm ... How are we to know if we are sexually compatible if we do not have sex with the person before we get married? "Oh, but you will learn together," they say, or "You will obey your husband," when it comes to sex. Not! We are the ones who get to decide what kind of sex we will have, not our spouses. We are the authority of our bodies, and we are the ones who determine if and when we choose to participate in any type of sexual activity.

Sex is treated like something dirty. We are taught from a young age that touching oneself is dirty, and children are shamed if they're caught exploring their own bodies. Rather than shaming children, what if we encouraged open and healthy discussion about sexuality? What if we educated children, and provided them with the information they need to grow into sexually-healthy adults?

Homosexuality has been around since the beginning of time. Many cultures and religions discourage it and say that to have sex with another person of the same sex is a sin or disgraceful. If two men or two women were to have sex, then they would not be able to have a baby, but does that really matter?

I remember talking about homosexuality at work one day. There was a woman who had approached the subject of people being gay and wanted to know our thoughts on the subject. A younger woman stated that she looked at people who were gay as just another form of love. It was a profound statement when she went on to explain that there are many types of love, such as love between parents and their children, between a man and a woman, between brothers and sisters and between cousins. Homosexuality is just another form of love. There are many different ways to love. So, if we love another, why would it be any different to show that love through sex, even if we are in a relationship with a person who happens to have the same sexual anatomy as us? Love is love.

I only have a few family members and friends who are part of the LGBTQ+ community. I am not well-versed in the terms associated with their culture. Again, my only concern is for those who are trying to live their lives by being authentic in who they are to have the love, support and acceptance in society. If you feel uncomfortable around others with different sexual preferences, then ask yourself why their life-style bothers you so much? Are you afraid of others knowing your sexual preference?

Love is often left out of the equation when it comes to teaching children about sex and sexuality. Love of self should be stressed as the most important part of sexual sovereignty. Many disempower us by teaching us that we are to follow other's rules on our sexuality, like many other areas of our lives.

Journal Questions

- Are you feeling stuck in gender roles? Do you feel more masculine or feminine at times which does not match your physical identity?

- How has society shaped your view of loving someone of the same gender as you?

- In what ways has society taught you to be ashamed of your body?

- If God/Universe is all-loving, then how can being in a romantic same-sex relationship be condemning?

- Men have translated the Bible over thousands of years: is there a possibility that those in power have manipulated the written work for their own agendas?

5

Fear/Beliefs

Fear ... What are we really afraid of? We have many fears and beliefs that we have been taught by our family, friend and society itself.

Individuals who are afraid, scared or jealous will try to control how you feel. Especially if they believe you are a threat to them or the things they want. Insecurity can produce strong feelings of fear. Fear of not having enough. Fear of others having things in their lives that they want. Fear of not being loved. Fear of being alone. Fear of someone younger coming along and taking what used to be theirs.

When we are little, we are taught what to believe by our family. Some people are taught that life is hard, money is evil, men are violent, and you must work hard for money, etc.

We are taught at a young age that you must be just like all your friends to be liked and accepted or cool.

Society has made us believe that if we are not tall, thin, beautiful, smart and successful, then we are not worthy. People base their self-worth on their social status. Thinking they must have the bigger house, new car and stylish clothes to feel successful and believe they are worthy.

When I really started to question my beliefs, I realized that none of them were my own. Everything I believed had been taught to me by someone else in my life. Every negative thing I was told about myself, I believed because, at one time, I had someone very strongly tell me what I believed was not real. From that day forward, I believed everyone else instead of listening to my own inner voice. Even though many things did not resonate with me, I still believed others over myself.

As children, we are taught to think like our parents, from how to treat others to our place in society. We believe when we are told we are smart or even when we are told we are not good enough. We are conditioned at a very young age to stop listening and believing what we think is true for ourselves.

I realize now that I did the same thing with my own children growing up. I discouraged things that I did not think were true because of what I was instructed to believe. I taught my own children the way of how things worked in the world. I taught them not only to be kind and respectful, but I did a great disservice to them by not listening to what they truly believed or what they were most concerned about. As parents, we often brush away children's fears by telling them there is nothing to be afraid of. Do you really take the time to sit and listen to not only the children in your life but to others as well?

I have found the reason that, most of the time, we are afraid to speak our truth or tell someone how we truly feel. It is because we are afraid of their reaction. I can look back now and see why I did not or could not tell someone how I was really feeling. I was afraid of their reaction. Were they going to get mad or upset? Would they get angry enough to physically hurt me? Would they leave me? Would they find me disgusting or revolting? Rejection and uncertainty can be powerful fears that keep so many of us stuck or unable to move.

A lot of people are afraid of being alone. Many associate being alone with being unlovable, or that there must be something wrong with them. Being alone is not the worst thing that can happen to a person.

Being with someone who does not treat you with love, kindness, and respect is worse. Know deep in your heart that you deserve better, and you are worth more than just putting up with someone who does not treat you with love and respect.

Do not let fear or uncertainty stop you. While life may get in the way at times and will oftentimes put some things on pause, you can always start again where you left off. As for myself, it has taken three years for me to complete this book. Lots of starts and stops for many different reasons, but when the time was right, I was again led to a publisher, obtained the money to get this book in print and to finally release it, all the while knowing deep down that since I was led to complete this project, then it is needed.

Even if this book only reaches a few people or as many as thousands or even millions of people, my only desire is that others recognize where they may have been taught to give away or believe they do not have personal power over their own lives.

It was once explained to me that fear is nothing more than not having all the information that everything will work out. If it does not work out, time is not wasted because you have gained experience from your efforts and know that you will be ok.

My wish for you is to be fearless, even it is one small step at a time. Eventually, all those small steps will lead to a point or goal that you would not have achieved if you had not started at all.

Journal Questions

- What are you truly afraid of? Being criti-cized or being made fun of? Physically injured?

- Are you afraid of the outcome? Why? What is the worst and the best that could happen?

- What if you fail at something? Oh, but what if you are successful? Do you have fears of being a success?

- Are you afraid of being rejected by family and friends? There are billions of people in the world, are you going to let a few people who may not accept you discour-age you from being or doing something you truly desire?

6

My Health Journey

During my search to help heal my physical body, I have searched, read and learned about many different modalities. Many of the things I learned were not common around the small-town area where I live. Many others I would talk to would say things or dismiss what I was learning because it was not mainstream. I was learning about herbs, essential oils and energy healing. Even my children, who were then in their teenage years, would often look at me like I had two heads. I was the weird parent because all the other parents were not discussing with their children different herbs that are good for sinus issues or to help you sleep or to fight an infection. I did not let them or anyone else deter me from finding what would work for me to help me feel better and to heal my body physically.

During that time, I learned many things which I am most thankful for. The most unusual and most beneficial along the way is Reiki. Reiki is what is known as "energy work." I will not go into detail here, but I would like to say that Reiki has helped me in so many more ways than just trying to physically heal me. You can google what Reiki is.

When I was "attuned" to Reiki, I was told that with it, there could be changes to my life. It was explained to me that things that are not for my "highest good" could possibly leave my life. I really did not understand what that meant at the time. I was attuned to the first two levels of Reiki in 2007. I mention this because, by the end of 2009, I had separated from my husband at the time. I did not put two and two together until I was attuned to the Master/Teacher level of Reiki in 2015. OK, call me a slow learner, lol. I was seeing someone off and on for a few years; in less than six months after receiving my Master level, the relationship ended abruptly.

The five years between 2010 and 2015, there were major changes in my life. Getting divorced, going back to college and getting my business degree, putting my youngest through college at the same time as me going to college, having a major health crisis and meeting many amazing women who would help me become who I am today.

The Reiki Master who conducted my level three attunements was a major factor in showing me the many gifts I have. Her name is Pam. I met her while I was working at an organic grocery store in our area. She could see in me that which I could not yet comprehend at the time.

Stephanie encouraged me to take a psychic development class. It was a beginner class. It was to help you to learn to connect and to recognize our own intuition that we all have. Many people call it a gut feeling or an urge to do something but not really knowing why. I was very hesitant to take the class, but Stephanie said she thought it would really help me. Well, I took the class. Wow!

The class was very interesting and had very simple instructions on listening to the "still small voice" that we all have. Of course, the trick is to quiet the mind so you can hear/feel the answer to what you are wanting to know. The teachers used various exercises to practice. They even had activities for us to work on with other students. It really was quite interesting and fun to learn how to listen to your own intuition for answers. For me, the scariest part was at the very end of the class. We were to give an actual "reading" to another student. WHAT?! I thought, "There is no way I can give another person a psychic reading." Well … I did, and I was accurate on several details.

After taking the level 1 class, I signed up for the Master level class. Level 1 was only six weeks long. The Master level was six months. Both of these classes have helped me in so many more ways about listening to my own intuition or higher self than I could have ever imagined.

So yes, I am psychic. I am also a medium. I know most people are probably saying, "Really?" or "Whatever, she had me until she said she was psychic." It really does not matter if you believe me or not. While being attuned to Reiki has opened (or should I say, re-opened) my abilities, this does not mean that everyone who is attuned to Reiki will become psychic or a medium. The only reason I am mentioning all of this is that, in this book, I will be talking about many of my experiences. Some of them may include some of the things I have gone through or experienced with my gifts.

At the time I started writing this book, I was 52 years old. It was difficult for me at first to accept the fact that I could have these abilities and not know about them until I was almost 50 years old. What the hell?! Is this some kind of joke the Universe/God is playing on me? Why wait so damn long? Well, the answer is because I am here as a teacher. I had to go through and experience a lot of different things in my life, so that now at this point in my life, I am here to teach others.

Along this path we call life, I have experienced many things, but as I look back on my life, even as I was growing up, I teach things I have learned, like math. I used to help others with their math homework. I was very good at math. Later in life, when I was learning about herbs and essential oils, at first, people would look at me like I was crazy, but sometimes years later they would start to ask about the things I would talk about on how herbs and essential oils could help with different things. Even my daughters, who thought their mom had lost her mind (lol), have asked me about the many "things you use to talk about." I remember the first time my oldest daughter called me and said, "I remember you talking about _____. Can you explain more about that? I remember you talking about it but don't remember the details."

I have had many health challenges, and each one has led me to learn more and more about different alternative treatments. I still try to do as many natural/ homeopathic remedies as possible before contacting a doctor. While doctors have their place, I think society has convinced us that doctors know more about us and our bodies then we do. Meditating and really listening/feeling how your body feels in any given moment can actually bring awareness to what you are feeling and why you may be feeling the way you do.

Journal Questions

- Have you taken the time to really listen to your body and what it needs?

- Do you take your health seriously? Do you ignore your body's signs and symptoms that something is wrong? Do you believe that you are too young and that you will not have any health issues until you are much older?

- Have you been taught to put yourself last? Why not put yourself as a priority, so you are able to help others better?

- Do you believe everything doctors tell you? Have you ever been told something by a healthcare professional that did not feel right in your own body (intuition)?

- Are your doctors really listening to you when you have a health concern? Do you feel like they are rushing you or just not hearing what you are telling them?

7

Resistance From Others

I know most of you are probably thinking, "If I start taking my power back from others, I will get resistance." Yes, you will.

Many people will avoid conflict to keep the peace. In reality, by not speaking up and saying something, you continue to give others your power. You shut down or repress your authentic self. We are not placed in this time and space to play small. We are so much more then we have been taught. Society has instructed us that we need to act, talk and conduct ourselves in a certain way, and when we start to behave differently, those around us will most likely start questioning our actions.

I have found sometimes that by speaking up and saying something, you will get a laugh from the other person. Some may laugh because they are surprised you have said something, but others will laugh because they have made you aggravated enough to speak up. The latter, I noticed, feel powerful because they were able to provoke you into a response. This is their ego deriving pleasure from your frustration. They want you to feel smaller and them to feel bigger.

I have had this happen many times with family. While at a family picnic and my mother and I were grilling food, I had a family member say very sarcastically that I could not cook. Instead of ignoring it, I made a comment back to him. He laughed, thinking it funny. The bigger story is this person has made comments like this my whole life. While I know, deep down, he really cares about me and has shown it in the past, there are many times when he thinks he is much better at doing things than others, not just with me.

Resistance can take on many forms from lots of people in our lives, especially our spouses. Living together, especially after several years, we have established a routine and expectations from each other. Life changes can be challenging when they disrupt our lives and cause lots of stress.

I remember the stress of losing my job due to the company closing the manufacturing plant I had been working at for almost ten years. My husband at the time was extremely upset because he felt he would need to take on more of the financial responsibility. While I understood it would be difficult for a short time, I felt that I could finally go back to school and become a massage therapist. I researched for schools in the area; I toured the colleges and applied to the one I felt would be a good fit for me. All I needed was to figure out how I was going to pay for it. When it came time to apply for money to pay for the classes, my husband got really upset and demanded that I get another full-time job and refused to listen about my dream or desire to go back to school. I was extremely upset and frustrated. We argued about it for a long time, but in the end, I went back to work and did not get my chance to fulfill my dream. This put a strain on our marriage, and six years later, we were divorced. Many other things happened within that time, such as my yearning to do the things I felt I needed to do for myself.

I was not born just to work, raise children and be a servant to my spouse. I was longing for a more meaningful life, and I could no longer take a back seat to the things I knew deep down that I was meant to accomplish in this lifetime.

Yes, you will get resistance from others, especially those who may be the closest to you. In the end, the people that really love and support you will continue to be a part of your life. Those that leave have served their purpose of teaching us lessons. Wish them well, as they are on their own personal path. That path may have included you for a little while, but it has come time for each of you to go your own separate ways as you continue to grow and expand in your knowledge and power.

We would not grow if we did not have resistance. Stepping out of our comfort zones helps us to grow a little at a time and gives us the confidence to do it more and more. We may struggle and feel unsure, but with time and a little bit of practice, you will build your self-confidence and your personal power a little with each step.

Know that you will get resistance from others, particularly in the beginning. You may even lose family and friends over speaking up and doing things that are in alignment with who you truly are. It will be ok because, in the end, those who are meant to be in your life will stay, and others who are supportive of you will show up as well.

Journal Questions

- Are you afraid of the resistance you may receive from others?

- What types of resistance do you think you might get from someone?
  From family? Friends? Co-workers? Strangers?

- Do you think you will lose family, friends or your job for changes you want to make? Would you lose one or two people, or would you lose all of them?

- Would your life be better without certain people in your life because of their negativity towards you? It is not about if you can eliminate those people, but about if you are willing to let go of others that are keeping you down. Are you willing?

- Do you have people in your life that will support you and help you make the changes you want to make? Who are they? How much can you count on them?

* Are you afraid of being physically hurt? The only thing I can say if you are afraid of being physically injured is to have a safety plan in place, including support from others who will be able to help you in your time of need. Much love to you if this is your situation.

8

Other People Playing Victim or Rescuer

Once you really start owning your power and making choices to do only those things that you really want to do or have, you will start to notice others who play (or act) like they are victims.

Have you ever noticed how someone will say they do not have a choice to do or not do something? They say things like "I HAVE to spend time with my parent, even though I don't want to spend every Thursday night with him," or "We eat out at the same places all the time when all I really want to do is stay at home and eat in, but she wants to eat out so we will go out to eat." Really?!

Some people will say they don't want to do something but will turn it around and, with boastful pride, say, "No one can say I wasn't there for my parent because I spent every Tuesday with them, even when

I did not want to," or "I won't have any regrets because I spent time with Mom where everyone else was too busy or stayed away because they did not want to deal with their issues of losing Dad."

Listening to others complain and refuse to stand up for themselves or stand in their own power can be frustrating and very aggravating. There have been many times I just wanted to scream, "Stop being a baby about it and just say something!" Of course, most people would be offended by such a direct and accusing statement. Sometimes it works to be blunt, while other times, not so much. To keep your own peace of mind, you could gently suggest they try speaking up.

I have also heard others say that they "have to" help someone because "I am supposed to teach the other person what their true path is." I really do not understand that way of thinking. Feeling you do not have a choice in a situation is giving up your power. We all have the power to choose! Others may not like our choices, or we feel we are put on this earth to help/save others but is it true or is it only your perception? You cannot save others.

Others are not always going to like our decisions, and that is ok, but the final decision is always our own. Playing the victim is a choice. Feeling like you "have to" save others only puts the burden of other's decisions on you. You can either take your power back, or you can continue to give up your power by thinking you do not have a choice

Journal Questions

- Have you ever noticed those who play victims turn things around and blame others?

- Do you have someone in your life that is always complaining that things are always happening to them? Are they taking responsibility for their part of their "suffering?"

- Do you have people in your life who insist on helping others "because they have to?"

- Have you had someone try to blame you for their own mistakes and/or decisions in their lives?

- Do you feel they are trying to manipulate you or make you feel bad for making the choices that are best for you and your life?

9

I Don't Feel Like Smiling

We are often taught to hide our feeling to make others feel comfortable. Be true to your feelings. If you do not feel like smiling … DON'T.

I have often noticed that when a person is not feeling happy or they are depressed, most people will give them many reasons why they should not be feeling depressed or unhappy. Understandably, we want our family and friends to be happy and grateful for their lives and what they have, but truth be told, sometimes we just need to sit with our feelings to actually feel them.

Give yourself permission to feel your feelings no matter who is around. You can easily say that you are upset or even angry with someone without reacting to your feelings.

Feelings are like water. They ebb and flow daily as well as sometimes moment by moment. Our feelings can easily change based on what is going on around as well as those we are around.

Many of us have often woken up grumpy, sick or tired. We all have days where we just want to be left alone and other days that we are excited to be alive and feel like we can do anything in that moment.

While most of us can easily recognize why we are happy, being aware of what/why we are irritated is where true knowledge is at.

Honor your feelings when you are not in a good mood but learn to recognize the reason why you might not be feeling happy, are sad or even angry.

Try sitting with the feeling. I have found oftentimes, just taking the time to sit and acknowledge that I am not happy, even if it only for a few minutes, really helps to release the lower feelings. Take the time if you do not feel like smiling— don't.

Journal Questions

- Have you been taught to hide your feelings? Why?

- Were you taught to not bother others with your own problems?

- Do you push your feelings aside or avoid feeling them? Why?

- What would happen if you sat with those uncomfortable feelings? Can you spend just 5 – 10 minutes in those feelings?

- Are you afraid of looking weak and vulnerable?

- Have your tried journaling your feelings to help express them? You can always burn or throw away the pages so no one else will see them.

10

Thoughts ... Express Them
Any Way You Can

Have you ever been unable to sleep because your mind will not stop running the same thought through your mind? Thoughts will sometimes keep running through your head. I don't know about anyone else, but I find that if I cannot sleep because I have lots of thoughts or keep going over something in my head, the best way to get to sleep easier is to get up and write down what you are thinking about.

I have written many letters to people who have hurt me but never mailed them. There have been times where I have written a letter to express my feelings and thoughts to someone and was going to give it to them the next time I saw them, but by the time I saw them, I realized, in the end, it truly would not have mattered, or what I was fretting about had resolved itself.

Journaling has helped me to get a better understanding of things going on in my life. Many times, as I'm writing in my journal, the answers to my questions and/or concern will present themselves as I am writing. Remember, no one has to read what you have written in your journal. What you write is for you and you only. Of course, if you are worried or concerned that someone may see what you have written, then keep it in a safe place or even destroy the paper after you are done. I have done this a few times when I was really upset and angry with a person. I would write out what I was feeling in a letter addressed to them, and then I would take the letter outside and burn it while I asked the Universe to release the feelings of pain or hurt that I was feeling. I sometimes would also ask for forgiveness towards myself because we are often too hard on ourselves for things we have done or feel bad for having bad feelings towards another.

If you feel the need to cry while you are writing, that's ok too. I have written many words while crying. I have even written so fast that you were not able to read my writing. But in the end, it did not matter that what I had written was not legible; all that mattered was that I had gotten my feelings of pain, hurt and frustration out of me. There is power in the written word. Whether what you have written is published or not, expressing what you are thinking and feeling can give you the power you need to make it through another day. It can even give you the courage to stand up for yourself because only you can teach others how to treat you as you want.

We are much more than we give ourselves credit for. But we are always looking to others for approval, when all we really need is to be confident enough in ourselves to know that whether a person likes you or not has nothing to do with you but everything to do with how the other person is thinking or feeling about themselves.

So, go ahead and find a way to express your feelings. Try a couple of different things to see what works for you. Maybe even go back and forth between a couple of various modalities.

Journal Questions

- Have you thought about expressing your feelings? Are you afraid to express them?

- Do your thoughts and worries keep you up at night? Do they make it hard to concentrate on other things??

- How many different ways can you come up with to express your thoughts? Writing? Recording them? In art?

11

Pain ... Acknowledge It,
Feel It and Let It Out!!

Pain can show up in many different ways, such as anger and impatience as well as anxiety. Pain and hurt are mostly unexpressed trauma. While trauma is mostly seen and something major happening to a person, sometimes a small incident to a child can leave a lasting impact on the individual. Such examples might be not soothing a child when they are crying or not trying to figure out why they are upset. Even not attending a children's sports activity can make a young person feel like they do not matter to a parent or other important adult in their life.

If you are often frustrated with something, try taking some time to sit down and figure out why it is bothering you so much. An example might be why you feel others do not do something the same way you do, and you feel they are stupid or just plain ignorant. In reality, no one is smarter than another person. We have all been taught differently. Just because someone does not know how to fix an air conditioner or even fix a car does not mean they are stupid. The person has never been taught those skills. Would you think an average person is less intelligent because they do not know how to perform surgery?

The first step to healing is learning to acknowledge that you are feeling a certain way about something that is bothering you. Many people deny they are hurt or that something is bothering them. I have also observed others blaming someone else for their irritation or frustration. "If so and so had not done that thing, then I would not be upset." If you are upset or even uncomfortable about something, see if you can figure out why.

Is it because society has taught you that something is not acceptable? Of course, hurting another person or destroying/stealing something should not be tolerated but what I am discussing is something as simple as a little boy playing with dolls. Why does a boy playing with a doll bother you? Is it because society has set a standard that boys do not play with dolls? Why not? Are you afraid that a boy playing with a doll is going to make him gay? I know many women who would like or expect the men in their lives to help with children. How are men supposed to help with a child if they are not taught?

Give yourself permission to feel pain or discomfort about something. I have come to notice many people will bury or deny they are in pain or uncomfortable. Over the years of working with people, I have observed many immediately discard the notion that something is wrong. Many cultures have taught, especially to men, that if you show any type of vulnerability, others will take advantage of you. I believe those actions are from a time when survival was a necessity in the wilderness. Most countries have evolved into more civilized societies where immediate danger is seldom the case.

Breaking the habit of denying how you feel in the moment will take time. Do take a few moments later to focus on why you felt discomfort, especially if it was a very strong feeling. Understanding why can help free the restraints of feeling powerless.

Do not hold in the pain. Unexpressed pain will always find a way to be expressed or released. Working with counselors and therapists has given me insight into the many different ways to express pain and hurts as they surface. A couple of those I have noticed that can be very helpful are drawing pictures or writing out what you are thinking and feeling.

Also, do not be afraid if feelings of anger or sadness come up while performing any of the activities you have chosen to express your feelings. Remember, no one has to see or read what you have done. You can always destroy the picture or pages you have written. I speak more on expressing your pain in another chapter.

Pain, hurt, or feelings that have been denied keep you from being happy. Ignoring our feelings will not make us truly happy.

Over the years, I have found that crying is my way of releasing all kinds of negative, painful or unexpressed feelings. In the beginning, I would cry so hard and so long that it would physically hurt. My head would ache, and my throat would be sore. At times I would scream so hard I could not talk after. Sometimes, I would scream into a pillow, not wanting my neighbors to hear me.

The funny thing about unexpressed feelings of hurt or anger is that there were many times I did not understand why I was crying. It would oftentimes drive me crazy trying to figure out exactly why I was so upset and crying so hard. Once I realized that it was just my way of releasing all of those unexpressed thoughts and feelings, and I stopped trying to figure out why, it was much easier for me to accept that there was truly nothing wrong. I/my body needed to release that which no longer was serving me and my highest good.

Pain can be from not feeling you are/were being heard as a child. I can remember crying after something that had happened to me when I was no more than four years old and crying, but my parents and grandparent just kept telling me to stop crying and to lay down for a nap. I was in the other room from where they were. I was not able to properly express my feeling and felt very abandoned. As I look back now, I can see where I would do things to get attention. Not some of my proudest moments, especially as a teenage girl. Wanting people to like me because I thought I was not worthy unless I was liked.

Over time I have come to relax when I feel the need to cry. I could be watching a movie or listening to a song and shed a couple (or a lot) of tears. I do not try to figure out why because, in the end, it really does not matter why but know that whatever it is, it is ok. I will not lie and say that you will never cry again because that would be unrealistic. I have cried happy tears, aggravated tears because something is not working out the way I want, as well as many sad tears over the loss of someone close to me.

Cry if you must. Cry into a pillow. Even punch the pillow and cry if that is what you feel you need to do so you can let out that which is needing to be expressed so you can move on to happier times.

Journal Questions

- Are you pushing painful feelings down, ignoring them or denying them? If so, why?

- How many different ways can you find pain showing up in your life? As anger? As frustration? Being impatient?

- What is the real reason behind your pain? Because you are disappointed? Feeling unworthy? Feelings of being rejected or unloved?

- Do other people's actions or decisions bother you? Why? Are you uncomfortable watching or seeing someone do something?

- Are you experiencing discomfort because others are not following what is considered 'normal'? Is it hurting other people, animals or the environment? If not, then why does it bother you?

- What ways can you find to express your pain and discomfort? What about writing, painting, working out, gardening, or even building something? What about tearing something apart? Do you have something that is no longer useful and needs to be discarded anyway?

- Are you giving yourself permission to feel? Are you taking the time to really feel your feelings? Maybe cry or even scream out in frustration? Please make sure you warn others that might be around and not just yelling at others out of frustration.

12

Don't Let Others Tell You What You Are Thinking and Feeling!

I am not talking about being an a$$. While taking into consideration what other people think is good, and their opinions of what you are feeling or thinking can give insight into something you may not have thought of before, as we grow and learn to trust what is true for us we will come to recognize when others are trying to control or disempower us. Many times, they will do this out of fear – fear of you getting more than them or becoming better than them at something.

The reason I say not to let others tell you what you are feeling or thinking, or try to explain to you your reasons for doing something is that I have found, most of the time, well-meaning people (social workers, therapist, counselors, or even family and friends) are struggling with issues of their own.

I have been on this journey of learning to understand my own thoughts, feelings, and what is true for me, to find my own power and strength in all that I do, so it was a moment of great insight when one of my co-workers cut me off when I was explaining a situation. She told me the way I responded to what was happening was because I was taking offense to what was being said. When again tried to finish talking, she again interrupted, cutting me off. It was at that moment I realized she was telling her story of pain and hurt but was also trying to disempower me by telling me how I was feeling, according to her. I know the reason I said what I did, and it was not the reason she was insisting it was.

My co-worker has stated she has many issues and needs to work on them, which is good, but I have also learned that she uses subtle ways of saying or doing things to try to control things and people in her life. At that moment, when she was trying to tell me why she thought I was responding to the situation, I realized that it was her perception of what she thought was my reasoning, but in fact, it was what she was taught.

Now I understand that people live in fear and use different methods to control their lives. Parents have oftentimes used fear to control their children. Companies have used fear of being fired to control the employees. We will not even talk about the government or religion on ways and why they try to control us and our lives. We look to the "experts" to tell us or show what we should be doing or feeling, or even thinking. When we do this, we are giving our power and control over to others who do not have our best interests at heart.

Yes, we all live in a world that can be cruel at times, but I have also seen many beautiful people and things that make my heart sing. What makes me happy and the things that I see that are beautiful can be very different for each and every one of you. Does that make me right and you wrong? No, only you can truly know what you are feeling and thinking.

So how do you get to know what your true feelings are? For me, I have come to know my inner self by asking myself lots of questions. Clearing your mind of what others think and quieting your mind so you can hear your own inner voice. Learning to get past what others think of you and learning to think for yourself. For me, I have learned that doing Qi Gong and meditation every day has helped me to listen to what is true for me and only me. I will discuss mediation more later in this book.

To truly know what is right for us is to not let others tell us what is right. Even Me! ☺ Going within will help you to connect with who you truly are and not who we have been told we are and how we should feel or what we should think about things in our lives or the world around us.

Journal Questions

- Have you ever noticed someone dismiss or try telling you that your feelings were wrong?

- When someone is upset or angry, do they continue to defend themselves by trying to say that your feelings were wrong? Have you done this yourself?

- Have agreed with others only because you were unsure of how you felt about something to only realize later that your true feelings were different?

- Have you thought about doing a little research of your own on different subjects and deciding on your own how you feel about something?

- Do you let only the news, social media and 'experts' provide information on an important issue for you and your family?

13

Speaking Your Truth

To be true to who we are, we must embrace that which we are. Speaking up for what we believe is often discouraged. Many times, those around us want us to be who they think we should be. Change, for many people, is difficult because it causes uncertainty. What if you express your dislike for something that everyone else likes or even loves? Will they think you are strange? Weird? Not right in the head?

Following the crowd does not make us happy. We must learn what is right for us and us alone. Going against that which we have been taught can be difficult and scary as family and friends have come to expect certain things from us. They love us, but they want us to be who we have always been or expect us to be.

Now I am not saying that you need to be loud and obnoxious about your difference of opinions. I have noticed that as long as most people are in agreement with a subject, whatever it might be, that others are calm, and the conversation flows smoothly. When an individual expresses a different view, I have noticed, at least here in the United States, that others take a stance on certain topics with fury. I have seen friendships and family not speak to each other or downright disown them because their views are different.

Obviously, if we feel strongly about something, particularly if it is in reference to someone being hurt or other types of injustice, we will all be confronted with others who do not agree with us. You do not have to let the difference of options keep you from expressing what truly matters to you as an individual.

Just because someone has a difference of opinion does not mean that person is wrong, and you are right. It is simply another point of view. Attacking another person for a perspective that is not the same as their own is destructive and can become a tug of war for power.

Speaking your truth does not have to be a power struggle with others who do not agree with you. If someone is arguing their point, you have the power to choose to engage in the battle or simply to disengage and accept that not everyone is going to see things or believe things as you do.

Journal Questions

- Are you afraid to speak your truth? What are you afraid of?

- Do you believe having difference of opinions means you cannot be friends or associate with people with other viewpoints than yours? Why or why not?

- Are you able to accept that people have a whole range of perspective that is different from yours? Why or why not?

- Are you able to discuss an issue without getting angry with the other person? Why or why not?

- Are you willing to be open to other possibilities or willing to change your perspective? Why or why not?

14

Not All Relationships are Forever

I know! I know! But ... the Bible tells me so! What if we did not come here to find "the one" person we are meant to be with for the rest of our lives? What if we really came here on earth to have love and compassion for others? What if some relationships are designed to show you where you need to grow personally, professionally and maybe even spiritually? Life could be so much easier if we learned from each person we came in contact with. That includes the good, the bad and the ugly parts that no one wants or is willing to talk about.

I do believe that some relationships are meant to be forever, but not all. I see so many people in relationships that are not only not healthy but abusive. Yes, you may think, "well, why doesn't the person just leave?" Society does not make it easy to get divorced on many different levels.

Getting divorced can be expensive, especially for those who do not have a lot of money. Unless the couple agrees on how things will be divided with little-to-no disagreements, the process will take longer, which means more paperwork and time in the court systems, which equals the cost of divorce being much higher. My ex-husband disagreed with several items, so not only did it take longer for the divorce to be finalized, but it also ended up costing both of us more in the end.

With so many people owning homes and other property together, it can be challenging to decide what items each person is going to keep. If the item is a big purchase item, the next question is if there is money still owed on the loan taken? Many people will argue that they paid for the item because they are the one working, or paid for it out of the earnings they brought home.

On top of everything else, you have family members, friends and even society trying to tell us that marriage is sacred and should be worked out. This is not always an option. What most people do not realize is what goes on behind closed doors. When anger, jealousy, insecurity and infidelity are present, many things can and oftentimes do happen. Because people are taught not to discuss the problems in their marriages and many times did not have a good role model for what a happy and healthy relationship looks like, they often struggle on how to handle things and how to discuss their feelings, wants, needs and expectations.

Next is the cost of living as a single person. In many areas, especially here in the United States, one person working full time cannot always afford to live alone without a job that pays much more than minimum wage. It is even more difficult if you have children and have to pay for childcare, which can be particularly challenging if you have more than one child.

Parents and other family members should be a support system for each other. Many times, the stress, mental illness, societal pressures, peer pressures as well as expectations can often lead people to treating family members badly. Societies have not properly taught individuals how to handle or deal with stress along with healthy ways of dealing with the challenges of life and everyday living. People that are hurting emotionally often lash out and hurt those around them, especially those closest to them.

There is so much pain and hurt in many people, and the relationships they are in are only causing more pain/hurt not only to themselves but also to other people. Learn to recognize when a relationship needs to end. It does not matter if it is a friend, family or romantic relationship; it is time people sit down and take a good look at each relationship in their lives and decide if it is healthy, supportive and workable, or if it is destructive, appalling and nasty.

Healthy relationships, while they occasionally have issues, are mostly engaging, empowering, and rewarding. I don't know about anyone else, but I want people in my life who are supportive and encouraging yet are not afraid to speak up and tell me the truth if that I have said or done something that might not have been considerate or hurtful. We are all human and do not always see the different ways we may be causing others pain.

Journal Questions

- Do you still have all the same friends from when you were in school?

- Those who have been married for many years: are you truly happy? Does your spouse support you in all areas of your life?

- Have you ever had a friend that you thought was so close that you never thought anything would come between you, to only years later stop talking? Why? Was there a life lesson you learned from that relationship?

- Are your current relationships with family and friends healthy? Are they supportive of your decisions? Why or why not?

- Are there any relationships that are toxic? Is it causing you emotional, physical or mental pain? If it is, why do you continue to talk or spend time with the other person/people? Is it because you always have?

- Are you willing to limit your time with those who do not have your best interest at heart?

- Do your relationships have the same values, morals and priorities? Are they at least considerate of what is important to you? Especially if it's different than what's important to them?

15

Getting Along and Doing What is Best for the Children

I don't know about people in other countries, but here in the United States, many couples, when their relationships end, hold on to their hurt and pain. If they have any children, they often will continue to fight, argue and/or talk bad about the other person in front of or to the children. What good does it do? In reality, you are only hurting the children, possibly more than when you and your ex were together.

Especially young children who do not like to see their parents fighting. Many times, the child(ren) will think or feel like it is somehow their fault parents are not getting along. Even as they get older, children can frequently think, "If I was good, then my parents would not fight or would still be together." Children often are not able to understand why their parents are arguing, being mean or saying nasty things to each other.

While you may have every reason in the world to be mad, hurt, upset, angry and downright pissed off at your ex-spouse or family member, if you act out on those feelings then your actions are teaching children that it is acceptable to hurt another person, whether it is physically, emotionally or mentally.

As for myself, when my first husband, Frank (not his real name), and I got divorced, we decided early on that no matter our differences, we would work together for what was best for our two daughters. Our two girls were only four and two years old when we got divorced. While there were many times I could have expressed my anger and frustration in front of them, I instead chose not to do it. My reasoning for keeping my personal feelings and opinion of their father to myself was because I wanted them to have a loving relationship with their dad. Even though I did not agree with his drinking issues, I also knew that if he did not change, that as the girls got older, they would see for themselves that he had a drinking problem. We had many other issues besides drinking that lead to us getting divorced. I am using drinking as an example.

As the girls got older and would mention my ex's drinking and other things they did not understand, I did not speak negatively about him. I was there for them and supported them the best I could. I told them I understood their confusion about why he drinks so much. I could have told them story after story of the things he had said or did when he was drunk, but it would not have helped them to understand or improve their relationship. If I had told them all of those things, I believe it would have hurt not only them but their relationship with their father.

Over the years, with the girls traveling back and forth between my home and their dad's home, they have seen us attend a family wedding on his side, meet for lunch while dropping the girls off, and be around each other many times. While we remained friends and supported each other in our own lives, we always made sure that we talked and did what was best for our daughters.

Both girls are now in their 30s and, for the most part, have a loving relationship with their dad. As with all relationships, we have all had our ups and down with each other. Even now, they do always agree with me or their dad on our life decisions, but they are able to understand about life choices that we have to make each and every day.

Now, as for me and my second husband, George (not his real name) and our daughter ... Well, that is a slightly different story about getting along. Again, I did not say anything bad about her dad. We divorced about the time our daughter was three years old. By this time, my older two girls were eight and six years old. At first, we seemed to be ok with separating and getting a divorce, but it did not take but several months or about a year for things to get a little heated whenever we talked. George would get frustrated because our daughter would not talk to him on the phone. I really tried to get him to understand that at the age of three or four, a child does not comprehend talking on the telephone.

I remember George and I had a heated argument over the phone. Our daughter was visiting him at his home in Texas at the time of the disagreement. When he returned our daughter to my home in Ohio, we still were not talking much at all.

As I have said before, all relationships can go through difficult times. While it was challenging for George and me to get along, even for the sake of our daughter, he was not getting along with his parents as well. Within a few months, my ex-father-in-law, James, called me and stated that they had had a disagreement with George. James stated since George was not coming home to visit them that they would not be able to see their granddaughter. I can remember James stating he did not want him and George's issues to cause issues between us. I explained to

James that the difficulties between George and me and the issues between George and them have nothing to do with my relationship with them and their granddaughter. James stated he was glad to hear that and wanted to know if they could come to Ohio and pick up their granddaughter so she could get to know their side of the family. I said, "Absolutely yes!"

James and my ex-mother-in-law, Alice, came to Ohio many times over the years to pick up and drop off my daughter. They would come at Christmas time, Spring Break and Summer Break from school. Many times, they would question if it was ok. They were concerned about my youngest being away from me so much and also not wanting to cause any more difficulties between George and me. I explained several times that I did not think it would be fair to my daughter if she did not have a relationship with her dad's side of the family. I felt and still feel children need to know both sides of the family. Of course, if there are safety issues, then I would limit time spent with their family, which would include anyone that is family or not.

My youngest daughter will tell you that some of the happiest times were spent with her grandparents, aunts, uncles and cousins. Because I was able to put my daughter and her well-being first and foremost, she learned a lot from her dad's side of the family. James became a father figure to my daughter throughout the years when her dad was not able to be there for her like she needed. James and Alice were very supportive to me throughout the years and even told me many times they were proud of me for how I was raising all three of my girls, not just their granddaughter.

Has it been easy getting along with people that are no longer family? Yes. While safety is always an issue, I would never be mean or disrespectful out of spite. We don't do our children any good by not teaching them that even though things didn't work out, it does not mean you cannot at least get along for the sake of the children.

Throughout the years, I always made sure my girls' dads and grandparents were included as much as possible in what was going on in the girls' lives. Each time the girls got a school picture or sports picture, I made sure their dads and grandparents also got pictures. Even when we were not getting along, I made sure pictures were sent, so they constantly saw how the girls were changing and growing up.

As for George and me, I can say that it has taken us many years, but we are now at least getting along. Our daughter got married a few years ago at the time that I am writing this. While I had not spoken to or seen George for many years, at the rehearsal dinner before the wedding, we did briefly speak and talk with others in conversation. After dinner, several of us went out and hung out for a couple more hours. Again, we talked a little more. Nothing really important and certainly not about us! Our daughter told me the next day while we were getting ready for the wedding that her dad was surprised I had spoken to him. I reminded our daughter that our differences were a long time again and were in the past. I told her that I forgave him a long time ago and only wished him well. She laughed because she already knew that I had no animosity towards her dad. Disappointed at some of the things he did or did not do while she was growing up, but again that was all in the past.

While we talked more at the wedding reception, I was most surprised when we were leaving that George stated he was astounded that I was not still mad or upset with him. I told him that it was a long time ago and that I had forgiven him many years ago. George stated he would like to text me some time but did not think our daughter would give him my number. I laughed and stated that if I told her it was ok, then she would give him my cell phone number. What shocked me the most was when he was getting ready to get in his truck to leave, he asked if he could get a hug. Yes, I gave him a hug and wished him safe travels as he was going back home, which was several states away.

The next day, George texted me and said that he still had my number in his phone and asked if he could call me. We talked for about three hours. He was still driving and had many hours before he would be home. We talked about many things during that time, but most of all, we were able to talk and heal that which I wish we could have done 23 years ago when we separated. As many people know, it takes time and effort to take a really hard look at your part of the issue and admit your own shortcomings in relationships.

The wedding was very healing for many people. Even though James passed away several years ago and was not able to physically be at the wedding, he was there in spirit. I was told before the wedding that George had a disagreement with his mother Alice and one of his sisters. I had reassured George's sister that we would take every precaution to make sure any disagreements were not brought up while at the wedding. In the end, I believe George and his family were able to come to a little bit of understanding, and my hope is that everyone continues to get along despite differences of opinions.

Note here, George has now been sober for six years and told me he now realizes that alcohol was a large issue with many of his relationships, not just with ours.

Children learn from others around them but mostly from their parents. While we may get angry and frustrated with our ex-spouse/partner, it is important that we provide good examples when it comes to dealing with someone you might be mad at or hurt by. The hardest part is keeping your emotions under control while the other person may be trying to fight or argue with you, especially in front of the children. Keeping children from their other parent because you are upset or angry at the other parent is not fair to the children. As I have said before, if there is a safety issue, then of course, speak about the safety concern.

We cannot control what others may say or do, but we can be an example to all children around us, not just with our own children, that even if they are no longer in a relationship with another person, they can still get along and work together for the well-being of all involved.

Journal Questions

- Are you able to get along with your ex-partner, at least in front of the children? Why or why not?

- Do you speak negatively about your ex-partner in front of the children? Why or why not? How do you think it affects them?

- Do you and your ex-partner attend school activities together? Are you able to attend activities and show united support?

- Are you able to heal any hurt between you and your ex? Have you tried? Why or why not?

- Have you taken steps to at least heal your own wounds from a relationship that did not work out? Why or why not?

- Can you forgive not only your ex-partner but also yourself? If not, is that pain hurting other relationships in your life?

16

Work or Play

Ok, we all know that we are supposed to do some type of work to pay the bills. What if what we really want to do for work is out of the ordinary, such as being an artist of some kind? I have heard many times that being successful as an artist is not real work, and you cannot make enough money to survive. Why not? There are many who have started small and have worked their way to making a thing they like or love to do into a very successful small business. All you have to do is look on the web to see a multitude of entrepreneurs who are happy doing something they love while providing services or products to others.

My solution for doing the things that I really want to do or know that I need to do is to break it down into smaller pieces. We often make or think a project is so big in our mind that we let the fear or overwhelming feelings keep us from doing what we need to do.

You don't have to have it all figured out. Just take the first step and start with a few small steps.

Break it down. For me and writing this book; at first, it was a large project. I once heard an author who would write down little bits of ideas and inspirations down on whatever she had available to her at that very moment. "Ah Ha!" I thought, "I can do that with this book." So, for several weeks I would jot down different things that came to mind when writing this book.

I would still get nervous because I was trying to figure it all out before I actually started to sit and type my thoughts. Another thought that kept occurring to me was to stop trying to see the whole picture when all you really need to see is the next step. OK, OK. One day I realized that the Universe/God/Source had already started to put things in place for me to write. First, I saw a person on Facebook who was searching for authors who wanted help in self-publishing, then I took two writing classes, and I met someone who had done marketing and to top it all off, I mentioned to a friend of mine about writing a book, and she told me that she has a friend who does editing. Wow! Really?! Well, hell, I guess it is time for me to start taking the notes I have been writing down and to actually start to put them into this book.

While I used small steps to complete this book, you can also apply those same steps to anything, such as learning to paint. You could start watching videos or buy a few items, such as a few paintbrushes and small tubes of a few different colors. You could even begin by sketching.

The internet is filled with countless videos and information about almost any topic you can think of. Most libraries have books on hand that you can check out to read and study on almost any subject matter you could possibly imagine.

Even if your passion does not become a huge success or a full-time occupation, it can help you feel fulfilled on many different levels. For me and my book, my only hope is that it may help just one other person see that they have their own personal power to do the things that they truly want to do and to not let others negativity or doubts discourage them in pursuing their deepest desires no matter how small they might be. Start small. Remember, you do not have to have it all figured out before you begin.

My challenge to you is to do one small thing each day, whether it is researching or watching a video on any subject that you are curious about. Even if it is for only five to ten minutes a day, just ten minutes a day for six days is one hour of time spent learning.

Try it for just a couple of weeks. If you want to create something, then get just a few supplies and again spend a few minutes each day for a couple of weeks practicing what you have learned. Do not worry if life gets in the way, as it will at the times; just pick back up where you left off. In as little as one year, you will be so much farther than if you never started. Who knows, maybe at first you only sell a couple of your items, but maybe after a few months, your project really starts taking off.

Example: A classmate I went to school with started her own cookie business out of her home, at first to help her daughter pay for something at school. Even after they no longer needed the money, people continued to order cookies. Eventually, she quit her job and started producing cookies full time. The one thing that always struck me about her is that she said she would only continue to make cookies as long as she enjoyed doing it. Do what brings you pleasure, even if it is on a small scale.

Journal Questions

- Do you really enjoy your current job/occupation?

- Why do you stay working where you do? Are you happy there? Why or why not?

- Is there something else you would rather be doing for a living? If so, what small steps could you take towards your dreams?

- Do you know someone who is already doing what you want to do? If yes, could you talk to them about how they got started?

- If not, have you tried looking for some videos or read some books on the subject?

- What is the main reason you are not following your passion? Money? Lack of confidence? Worthiness?

- Why are you not trying? Is it because others are already doing it? Do they do it like you? Do they have your insight or unique style?

17

Defining Success

Society has come to a place where success is determined by material things, job status, educational degrees or how we look. Comparing each other by another's status only diminishes everyone's happiness.

Many people are not happy with their jobs or feel lonely at the top. I have watched people pursue a career because it will make them lots of money or will bring them great success in their field, yet after all the years of finally achieving what they thought would make them happy, they find themselves empty.

Society has become a place where if you are not successful enough, skinny enough, have the right house, job or car, you are not worthy. Have you let others decide for you what your worth is? How do you determine success in any areas of your life? We can let society determine our worth by the social class we are born into or by how tall we are or even by our physical or mental abilities, or we can decide for ourselves on what we are worthy of and we can determine what is successful and what is not for ourselves.

Life has become a competition, and many times we have been taught that there is not enough for everyone, so we must do whatever we have to do to make sure that we are not left behind, or someone else will get our piece of the pie. I have observed people not sharing, or withholding information, thinking that by doing so they will have the upper hand to get the job promotion or bid on a job they are hoping will make them more money or help them climb the corporate ladder. All because we have been taught that to be successful, others must have less than us.

The beauty industry has convinced the majority of society that they have to be young, beautiful and skinny to be attractive, and you need to be attractive to be successful. We see this every day in commercials, whether it is on TV or in a magazine.

When somebody feels as there are others who are more successful, oftentimes it leads to bitterness or resentment toward those who have achieved what is often perceived as success.

Define success for yourself. If being a parent since you were little is the only thing you have ever wanted, then having a child and being able to raise that little person makes you successful. The same can be said if all you desired when you were growing up was to run your own company, and now you have a thriving business. Let your definition of success for you be only yours. We all have the right to measure our accomplishments by our own standards. No one knows what it may have taken you to get where you are. Even if you have not obtained success yet, as long as you are doing the little things that will lead you to where you want to go, then you are prosperous each and every day.

What we want can also change as we get older. As a person, we are changed by our life experiences, which can often lead us to change what we thought was important and would make us successful.

We have been taught that to be successful, we must have a higher education, expensive clothes, a large house and an even more expensive vehicle, and only those things will make us feel we have succeeded in life. What if success to us is nothing more than a small little house with a job that you love surrounded by family and friends? Not that there's anything wrong with wanting a bigger house or fancier car, but what if the only reason you want those things is that you feel the pressure of the need to have it all in order to feel like you are successful?

We are all unique in our own individual ways, so why should we let society, parents, family, or friends determine what success means to us.

Money does not equal happiness.

What if we started to define success as doing things and having things that make us truly happy, no matter how big, small or expensive the stuff you have is?

Journal Questions

- What is your definition of success?

- Do you feel or believe that you have to work hard or at a high-paying job to be successful?

- Is work the only way you feel successful? What about money? Big house? Fancy cars?

- Are you looking to society or your culture to determine what success is supposed to mean to you?

- Do you place your self-worth on how much money you make/have or how many people you know?

18

This is Who I Am...
I Will Not Apologize!!

My name is Anna Williams. I was born in a small Northwestern town in Ohio. I am one of four children. I am the third child and the only girl. Both of my parents worked full time while I was growing up. Was raised Catholic. Graduated high school and went on with life as I thought I knew it.

I think, for the most part, I had a normal childhood. I liked to play with my brothers and their friends. We would climb trees and play in the cornfield behind the house where we used to live when I was younger. We lived on the edge of town and enjoyed playing hide and seek in the cornfield. Of course, as we got older, my brothers did not want their little sister to play with them anymore.

I don't think I had lots of girls as friends growing up because I got along with the boys better. I just did.

Not that I did not enjoy playing or spending time with other girls. I guess it was mostly that I did not feel comfortable with a lot of the other girls because they often judged me or others. Being "catty" is what most people would call it. Either way, I have found that as I have gotten older, the point of spending time with my girlfriends is that we support each other and are there for each other like it should be. I still get along with most guys better than women, but I am ok with that because the women I do have in my life are awesome! I cannot imagine my life without such strong and beautiful souls in my life.

As I was growing up, I also had many adults that would dismiss many things I would say as my imagination or just plain strange. It has taken me a long time to realize that what they disregarded was, in fact, many of my gifts. I could go on to tell you how a teacher squashed many of my ideas and really make me think that I was a fool or stupid for thinking the things I believed to be true. In the end, I have come full circle to finally see what is true for me and me only. While there are many others out there that will say they do not believe me and what I am about to say, along the way, I have had some amazing people show me that I am not crazy, and yes, it is true because they can see it too.

This journey has been long in the making. I have had many hard times and lessons to learn along the way before I would be able to come to where I am now in my life. Many of the women who are such a big part of my life have shown me many of my gifts and have confirmed them along the way.

What first started out as a search for my health issues at the time has taken many turns, as well as several ups and downs. What I thought was me trying to find a way to heal my body has actually been a spiritual journey to who I truly am in this life.

Like many girls, I grew up. Where I am slightly different is that when I graduated from high school, I joined the military and started a family while I was serving our country here in the USA. I spent a little over seven years in the Army. I did get to travel to Germany, which I had wanted to do since I joined the military. I had a little side trip to Saudi Arabia for Desert Shield/Desert Storm in 1991 for about five months before returning to Germany. In 1992 I decided to get out of the military, so I could be home with my girls. At the time, I already had two little girls and was pregnant with my third child, which was another girl.

In 1995, I left Texas where we had been stationed and returned home. Needing to support my family, I did what any other mother would do, I got a job and went on to raise my three girls. My girls have always been my pride and joy, as well as what has made my life truly worth living.

As with any other family, we had many ups and downs, but in the end, my girls know that I am always there for them, and I hope that I have made them proud of me for my accomplishments in life, just as they have made me proud to see who they each have become. I am also so very proud of my stepson and his family. While his father and I are no longer together, they have kept me as a part of their lives and the lives of their children. They may not be family by blood, but they will always be family in my heart.

I am different from most, but you know what? I am finding that there are many more people like me that have been afraid to express or show who they truly are because they are scared of what others will say to them or about them. We have been taught that to be different is to be criticized and/or disliked. We are taught that we are not worthy or good enough if we are different. If we were all the same, the world would be boring. We should celebrate that which is different and encourage our children to not only think outside of the box but to get rid of the whole damn box!

Journal Questions

- Do you let others opinions of you define who you are or who you should be? Why or why not?

- Growing up, was there a time you can remember that family or even friends dismissed you for being weird or strange? Are you able to look back now and see if their intentions were good or if they were trying to convince you that you should try to fit in and be like others?

- In what ways are you different from those around you? Do you hide your true authentic self? Why or why not?

- Do you feel you are too old to express who you truly are?

- Are you afraid of showing others the little things that make you unique?

19

Take Time to Enjoy Life

While you might think this is a no-brainer, there are many people who will not take time to enjoy even a simple cup of coffee. I mean, really sit down with a cup in hand and do nothing else. No list running through your head of what you need to do today or how silly it is to be wasting time sitting doing nothing.

Sitting and doing nothing is actually doing a lot. For me, it helps to meditate in the morning. It gives me a feeling and a sense of calm at the start of my day with a sense of peace. Now, it has taken me some time to learn to sit quietly and do nothing, but I have learned that I have more patience and am able to handle stress better when I take time to sit for a few minutes in the morning.

I can hear you say, "But I don't have time to meditate or sit still." What about five minutes in the morning? What about 10 minutes? Ok, so what about spending 15 minutes coloring or painting or even writing in a journal?

We have been taught that it is not ok to take time for ourselves because we have to do always be doing something or to be doing everything for everyone else. Especially mothers! Nourish yourself because you cannot pour from an empty cup. I know we have heard that saying many times, but it is so true.

I know I can hear all the mothers and fathers saying they don't have time because they are taking care of the children. How about including the kids in a little bit of fun as well? I, for one, wish I had done this more often with my own children. I did pass along the love of reading to my girls. They all love to read, even to this day. As I sit here, I am thinking, "I wish I would have taken more time to do other things such as painting, drawing, building more snowmen or sandcastles and taking nature walks while they were little." I wish I hadn't worried about the mess and focused more time on having fun. Having fun does not have to take a lot of time or money.

Even taking time to pamper yourself can help improve your overall happiness. Ok, men, this includes you. I personally get a massage once a month. Don't have money? Give yourself a foot massage or see if your partner will trade back massages. Men need to learn to relax too. I know many men who work long hours only to come home and fall asleep after 30 minutes because they just worked a 15-hour shift. Women work hard at work, too and then come home to the demands of their family. Take turns, if necessary, and help with the kids and doing things around the house. It only seems fair to me to help each other get the time to pamper themselves, to rejuvenate and fill their cup back up so they can continue to help others – and men, support your partners too if they are working. Women often work full-time and then spend many more hours after they get home doing more work around the home. Women need to feel supported by the men in their lives at home by helping around the house and with the children. Also, a reminder to the men, women need to feel supported emotionally, not just physically or financially.

While I enjoy meditating first thing in the morning, that is what works for me. For others, doing it in the evening or during lunch would be better. The time of day, I don't think, really matters as long as you take the time to enjoy something that brings you joy, excitement and happiness. I have taken painting classes, colored pictures, written in a journal, sang some of my favorite songs and danced like no one was watching in my kitchen while making brownie waffles. Try something you can do it anywhere and at any time. Make life fun. It really does make life better when you do things that really make you feel alive and happy inside as it melts the stress away of the things we tend to worry about, which in the scheme of things really are small things that try to steal our joy and happiness.

Take a little bit of time and go for it!

Journal Questions

- Do you take time to do the things that you really enjoy? Why or why not?

- Do you make time for yourself and your needs, not just your wants? Why or why not?

- Do you believe you can take just a few minutes each day to do something that you genuinely delight in doing? Why or why not?

- Have you actually taken the time to sit and consider what would bring more joy into your life? Why or why not?

- Have you been taught that you cannot take time to enjoy even the simplest things in life because of all your other responsibilities?

- Are you waiting until you have lots of money or when things settle down because life is too busy right now?

20

What if?

What if you started writing? Would you keep it a secret, or would you let others read it? How about reaching out to a publisher or two just to see if anyone is interested. You really never know if your story will resonate with another. It might even help them to know they are not alone in what they have gone through or how they feel.

What if you started doodling? Do you already draw? Do you like making jewelry? Is there anything you like to do or make? Try showing others your creations. You just might be surprised to see that others might actually like or even care about that which makes you feel good and empowered.

While dreaming of "what if," you will most likely have feelings of fear, frustration or even embarrassment. In reality, what is there to fear or even to be ashamed of? Wanting to be accepted in today's society is understandable, but why do you need to hide parts of you that society deems unacceptable for whatever reason they might say?

Women can be great leaders, just as men are capable of taking care of children. Boys are able to learn to cook and clean, same as girls are competent at repairing a vehicle. Societies and cultures have put so many people in boxes and many times with limits on what people should be doing instead of encouraging people to follow their dreams and desires.

Even if those with disabilities can still do things. They may need to adapt items or their way of doing things, but that does not mean those we often see as being unable to do certain things, in reality, could engage in activities they had always been told were out of reach.

Whether your aspirations are just for yourself and your family or to share them with the world, why not follow them? While I have written this book in the hopes of showing others how we have been taught that we are limited or should not be more than what others want us to be, my biggest hope is for others to stop and genuinely confront those parts of you and your life that others have told you that cannot or should not because .... (Fill in the blank).

Challenge: Do one small thing that you might be intimidated to do! If you are afraid of what others might think or say, then do it quietly at first until you become more confident.

Afterword

As with all thing we do, writing this book in itself has been a journey. It has taken many twist and turns a long with many ups and downs in the development of not only the idea of the book but the process to seeing it completed.

It really all started with journaling my thoughts, feeling and taking notice of people and situation around me. At first it was just a notebook and pen in front of me with not real intention other than to write down my day.

Some of the concepts I started to write about really started to make me wonder why people did or would not do certain things. Often when I would inquire to other on their reasoning for now pursuing some of their dream or even some of small things in their lives they would often give numerous reasons why not.

Some of the most common rationalities were because they were not smart enough, talented enough, not enough money but mostly they are either afraid of being criticized by other or society and cultural beliefs have taught people to feel they are limited and do not have the power to go after their true hearts desires.

For the longest time I thought to myself that there were already "so many" books on personal power and pursuing your dreams that what I perceived as just another book. I heard a statement several years that made me think 'why not me?'. That statement was 'there may be many books about the same subject but maybe the way you say it will be the way someone else need to hear it to understand the content.

When I first seriously started to consider submitting this book little things started to happen. Sometimes people around me positive while others though it was stupid. I learned quickly that often other who are negative about you creating something those are the ones most. Oftentimes those who do not want you to be more than them or they are projecting their fears on to you. I limited who I spoke to about my book for awhile to avoid becoming discouraged.

There were also little things that kept me going despite the negativity around me. Even though when a submitted a small story of my book to an online blog that were looking for stories and was refused because it was 'too. In-depth' for what they were looking for I would come across little things like coming across a publisher or company who does proofreading. While I did not contact the proofreading company for this book, I did contact the publisher. At that time I had only made little inquires into presenting a book. It would be a couple years later before I made a serious inquire after leaving a comment on one of his social media posts.

Even though the birth of this book has been a roller coaster of emotions and bumps along the way I decided to continue with it despite even my fears and limited beliefs. Why? If not me then who?

I have not merely lived these lessons but continue to work through limits that have been placed on my by others whether it is society, family, friends...even myself. We are all a work in progress as many of us step into our own personal power to truly pursue our own version of happiness and know that each of us not only have the power to go after what we truly want but that we are more than capable of achieving it.

It has taken many small steps to complete this book. I have fought through my own fears and insecurities. There were even days or weeks wear I did nothing with all of the pages I had written but I continued even when I thought I was done with the book and started to search for someone to publish it. I was lucky to come across this great publishing company again. I once more made another comment on this publishers social media where this time I did not let my insecurities stop me from accomplishing one small dream of getting this book out to show others they are not alone and that are more than capable and worthy of their true desires, whatever they might be.

About the Author

After growing up in Northwestern Ohio, Anna joined the military to experience the world beyond the small farming community. During her travels she observed many cultures and societal differences. Anna uses the accumulation of knowledge and direct observations as well as life experiences to help empower homeless veterans she works with. She returned to Ohio after leaving the US Army to raise her children and be closer to family. Anna enjoys reading, being out in nature and spending time with family and friends.

You can connect with Anna here:
Instagram **@anna.m.wms**
Facebook **@beingamoderndaymystic**

About the Author

Ellen Tovatt Leary spent twenty years acting on the professional stage. She performed in theaters from the Ahmanson in Los Angeles to the State Theatre in Lincoln Center, including four Broadway theaters (the Barrymore, the Lyceum, the Helen Hayes, and the Palace), and many Off-Broadway and regional theaters. She worked with Hal Prince, Maureen Stapleton and James Hammerstein among others. She graduated from Antioch College and was a Fulbright scholar at the London Academy of Music and Dramatic Art. Her first book, a memoir, *Mother Once Removed* details her childhood growing up on Bleecker Street in Greenwich Village in the 1940s with an eccentric, divorced mother. She was a staff writer at *Carnegie Hill News* in New York for fourteen years and has published short stories as well as poems. A native New Yorker, she currently resides with her husband in LA.

Acknowledgments

Thank you to the first readers and editors who generously gave their time and thoughts. These include Annie Levine Parker, Rebecca Leary Safon, Frank Hilf, Deborah Leary, Norman Parker, Barbara Coffey, Robert Sloane and Daniel Leary. I am in your debt.

Thank you to Karen Kondazian for her selfless support.

The Understudy would not have happened without the Los Angeles Writers Group who, chapter by chapter, spurred me on.

Thank you to my husband, David—my IT guy, my spell-checker, my sounding board, my Google searcher, my thesaurus, my driver, and my brilliant leading man, on stage and off, who knows all the stories I have to tell.